BOOK 3

FROM COLONIES TO COUNTRY 1735–1791

STUDENT STUDY GUIDE
TO THE REVISED THIRD EDITION

GRADE FIVE

OXFORD
UNIVERSITY PRESS

OXFORD
UNIVERSITY PRESS

Oxford University Press, Inc., publishes works that further
Oxford University's objective of excellence
in research, scholarship, and education.

Oxford New York
Auckland Cape Town Dar es Salaam Hong Kong Karachi
Kuala Lumpur Madrid Melbourne Mexico City Nairobi
New Delhi Shanghai Taipei Toronto

With offices in
Argentina Austria Brazil Chile Czech Republic France Greece
Guatemala Hungary Italy Japan Poland Portugal Singapore
South Korea Switzerland Thailand Turkey Ukraine Vietnam

Copyright © 2005 by Oxford University Press

Published by Oxford University Press, Inc.
198 Madison Avenue, New York, New York, 10016

www.oup.com

Oxford is a registered trademark of Oxford University Press

Writer: Ruth Ashby
Editor and Project Director: Jacqueline A. Ball
Education Consultant: Diane L. Brooks, Ed.D.
Design: designlabnyc

Casper Grathwohl, Publisher

Library of Congress Cataloging-in-Publication Data is available
ISBN 13: 978-0-19-976732-8

Dear Parents, Guardians, and Students:

This study guide has been created to increase student enjoyment and understanding of *A History of US*.

The study guide offers a wide variety of interactive exercises to support every chapter. At the back of the guide are several copies of a library/media center research log students can use to organize research projects and assignments. Parents or other family members can participate in activities marked "With a Parent or Partner." Adults can help in other ways, too. One important way is to encourage students to create and use a history journal as they work through the exercises in the guide. The journal can simply be an off-the-shelf notebook or three-ring binder used only for this purpose. Some students might like to customize their journals with markers, colored paper, drawings, or computer graphics. No matter what it looks like, a journal is a student's very own place to organize thoughts, practice writing, and make notes on important information. It will serve as a personal report of ongoing progress that a teacher can evaluate regularly. When completed, it will be a source of satisfaction and accomplishment.

Sincerely,

Casper Grathwohl
Publisher

This book belongs to:

_____

CONTENTS

Signing the Declaration of Independence was a bold and courageous act.

HOW TO USE THE
STUDENT STUDY GUIDES TO
A HISTORY OF US

One word describes A History of US: stories. Every book in this series is packed with stories about people who built a brand new country like none before. You will meet presidents and politicians, artists and inventors, ordinary people who did amazing things and had wonderful adventures. The best part is that all the stories are true. All the people are real.

As you read this book, you can enjoy the stories while you build valuable thinking and writing skills. The book will help you meet history-social science content standards and pass important tests. The sample pages below show special features in all the History of US books. Take a look!

Before you read

- Have a notebook or extra paper and a pen handy to make a history journal. A dictionary and thesaurus will help you too.

- Read the chapter title and predict what you will learn from the chapter. Note that often the author often adds humor to her titles with plays on words or **puns**, as in this title.

- Study all maps, photos, and their captions closely. The captions often contain important information you won't find in the text.

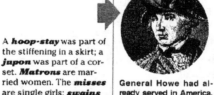

27 *Howe Billy Wished France Wouldn't Join In*

A **hoop-stay** was part of the stiffening in a skirt; a **jupon** was part of a corset. **Matrons** are married women. The **misses** are single girls; **swains** and **beaux** are young men or boyfriends. **Making love** meant flirting. **British Grenadiers** are part of the royal household's infantry.

General Howe had already served in America. In 1759 he led Wolfe's troops to seize Quebec.

Sir William Howe (who was sometimes called Billy Howe) was in charge of all the British forces in America. It was Howe who drove the American army from Long Island to Manhattan. Then he chased it across another river to New Jersey. And, after that, he forced George Washington to flee on— to Pennsylvania. It looked as if it was all over for the rebels. In New Jersey, some 3,000 Americans took an oath of allegiance to the king. But Washington got lucky again. The Europeans didn't like to fight in cold weather.

Sir William settled in New York City for the winter season. Howe thought Washington and his army were done for and could be

Swarming with Beaux

Rebecca Franks was the daughter of a wealthy Philadelphia merchant. Her father was the king's agent in Pennsylvania, and the family were Loyalists. Rebecca visited New York when it was occupied by the British. Her main interest in the war was that it meant New York was full of handsome officers:

My Dear Abby, By the by, few New York ladies know how to entertain company in their own houses unless they introduce the card tables....I don't know a woman or girl that can chat above half an hour, and that on the form of a cap, the colour of a ribbon or the set of a hoop-stay or jupon....Here, you enter a room with a formal set curtsey and after the how do's, 'tis a fine, or a bad day, and those trifling nothings are finish'd, all's a dead calm till the cards are introduced, when you see pleasure dancing in the eyes of all the matrons....The misses, if they have a favorite swain, frequently decline playing for the pleasure of making love....Yesterday the Grenadiers had a race at the Flatlands, and in the afternoon this house swarm'd with beaux and some very smart ones. How the girls wou'd have envy'd me cou'd they have peep'd and seen how I was surrounded.

126

As you read

- Keep a list of questions.

- Note the bold-faced definitions in the margins. They tell you the meanings of important words and terms – ones you may not know.

- Look up other unfamiliar words in a dictionary.

- Note other sidebars or special features. They contain additional information for your enjoyment and to build your understanding. Often sidebars and features contain quotations from primary source documents such as a diary or letter, like this one. Sometimes the primary source item is a cartoon or picture.

finished off in springtime. Besides, Billy Howe loved partying. And some people say he liked the Americans and didn't approve of George III's politics. For reasons that no one is quite sure of, General Howe just took it easy.

But George Washington was no quitter. On Christmas Eve of 1776, in bitter cold, Washington got the Massachusetts fishermen to ferry his men across the Delaware River from Pennsylvania back to New Jersey. The river was clogged with huge chunks of ice. You had to be crazy, or coolly courageous, to go out into that dangerous water. The Hessians, on the other side—at Trenton, New Jersey—were so sure Washington wouldn't cross in such bad weather that they didn't patrol the river. Washington took them by complete surprise.

A week later, Washington left a few men to tend his campfires and fool the enemy. He quietly marched his army to Prince-ton, New Jersey, where he surprised and beat a British force. People in New Jersey forgot the oaths they had sworn to the king. They were Patriots again.

Those weren't big victories that Washington had won, but they certainly helped American morale. And American morale needed help. It still didn't seem as if the colonies had a chance. After all, Great Britain had the most feared army in the world. It was amazing that a group of small colonies would even attempt to fight the powerful British empire. When a large English army (9,500 men and 138 cannons) headed south from Canada in June 1777, many observers thought the rebellion would soon be over.

The army was led by one of Britain's

General Burgoyne's redcoats carried far too much equipment. Each man's boots alone weighed 12 pounds. They took two months to cover 40 miles from Fort Ticonderoga to Saratoga, and lost hundreds of men to American snipers.

127

After you read

- Compare what you have learned with what you thought you would learn before you began the chapter.

The next two pages have models of graphic organizers. You will need these to do the activities for each chapter on the pages after that. Go back to the book as often as you need to. When you've finished each chapter, check off the standards in the box.

GRAPHIC ORGANIZERS

As you read and study history, geography, and the social sciences, you'll start to collect a lot of information. Using a graphic organizer is one way to make information clearer and easier to understand. You can choose from different types of organizers, depending on the information.

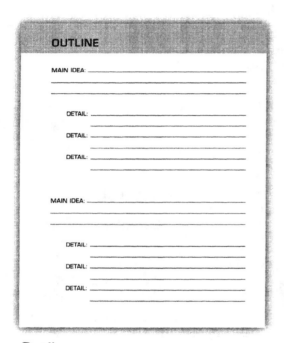

Outline

To build an outline, first identify your main idea. Write this at the top. Then, in the lines below, list the details that support the main idea. Keep adding main ideas and details as you need to.

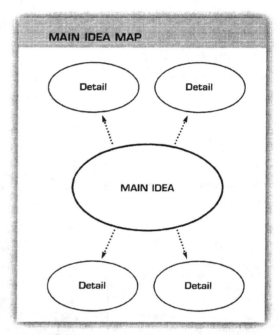

Main Idea or Concept Map

Write down your main idea or concept in the central circle. Write details in the connecting circles. You can use this form to make a word web, too.

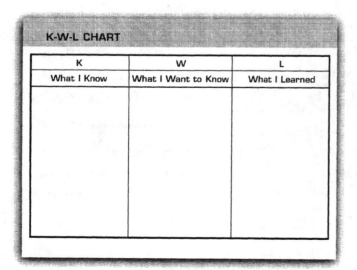

K-W-L Chart

Before you read a chapter, write down what you already know about a subject in the left column. Skim the chapter. Then write what you want to know in the center column. Then write what you learned in the last column. You can make a two-column version of this. Write what you know in the left column and what you learned after reading the chapter in the right.

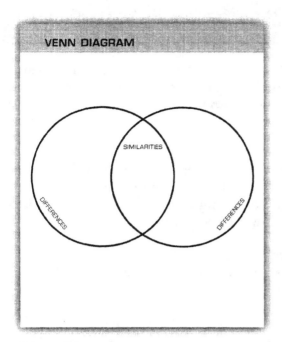

Venn Diagram

These overlapping circles show differences and similarities among topics. Each topic is shown as a circle. Any details the topics have in common go in the areas where those circles overlap. List the differences where the circles do not overlap.

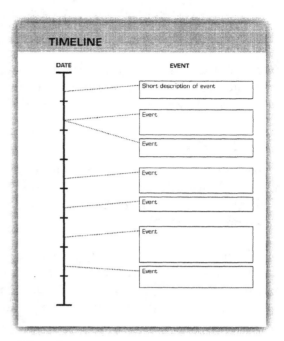

Timeline

A timeline divides a time period into equal chunks of time. Then it shows when events happened during that time. Decide how to divide up the timeline. Then write events in the boxes to the right when they happened. Connect them to the date line.

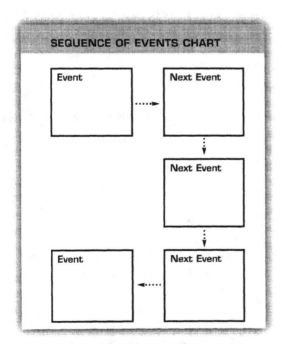

Sequence of Events Chart

Historical events bring about changes. These result in other events and changes. A sequence of events chart uses linked boxes to show how one event leads to another, and then another.

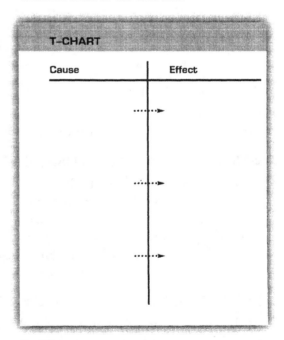

T–Chart

Use this chart to separate information into two columns. To separate causes and effects, list events, or causes, in one column. In the other column, list the change, or effect, each event brought about.

REPORTS AND SPECIAL PROJECTS

Aside from the activities in this Study Guide, your teacher may ask you to do some extra research or reading about American history on your own. Or, you might become interested in a particular story you read in A History of US and want to find out more. Do you know where to start?

GETTING STARTED

The back of every History of US book has a section called "More Books to Read." Some of these books are fiction and some are nonfiction. This list is different for each book in the series. When you want to find out more about a particular topic from the reading, these books are a great place to start—and you should be able to find many of them in your school library.

Also, if you're specifically looking for primary sources, you can start with the History of US Sourcebook and Index. This book is full of primary sources, words and evidence about history directly from the people who were involved. This is an excellent place to find the exact words from important speeches and documents. Ask your teacher if you need help using the Sourcebook.

DOING RESEARCH

For some of the group projects and assignments in this course, you will need to conduct research either in a library or online. When your teacher asks you to research a topic, remember the following tips:

TO FIND GOOD EVIDENCE, START WITH GOOD SOURCES

Usually, your teacher will expect you to support your research with primary sources. Remember that a primary source for an event comes from someone who was there when the event took place. The best evidence for projects and writing assignments always comes from primary sources, so if you can't seem to find any right away, keep looking.

ASK THE LIBRARIAN

Librarians are amazing people who can help you find just about anything in the library. If you get stuck, remember to ask a librarian for help.

WHEN RESEARCHING ONLINE, STICK TO CREDIBLE WEBSITES

It can be hard to decide which websites are credible and which are not. To be safe, stick with websites that both you and your teacher trust. There are plenty of online sources that have information you can trust to be correct, and usually they're names you already know. For example, you can trust the facts you get from places like pbs.org, census.gov, historychannel.com, and historyofus.com. In addition to free websites like these, check with your librarian to see which databases and subscription-based websites your school can access.

USE THE LIBRARY/MEDIA CENTER RESEARCH LOG

At the back of this study guide, you'll find several copies of a Library/Media Center Research Log. Take one with you to the library or media center, and keep track of your sources. Also, take time to decide how helpful and relevant those sources are.

OTHER RESOURCES

Your school and public library have lots of additional resources to help you with your research. These include videos, DVDs, software, and CDs.

FREEDOM OF THE PRESS
JENKIN'S EAR

SUMMARY The libel trial of Peter Zenger in 1735 helped established freedom of the press and the right to trial by jury in the American colonies. The War of Jenkins' Ear began decades of conflict between Britain, France, and Spain for control of North America.

ACCESS

A newspaper contains news, editorials, longer stories called features, and advertising. They are published either daily or weekly. Discuss with a parent or partner what different newspapers are published in your community. Why do you think more than one newspaper is published in an area?

WORD BANK   lawyers   apprentices   indentured servants

Choose words from the word bank to complete the sentences. One word is not used at all.

Boys in colonial America often became _____ for seven or eight years in order to learn a

trade. Other children and adults worked as _____ to pay off a debt.

CRITICAL THINKING

CAUSE AND EFFECT Make a line between each cause and the effect it made happen. Then read the matched pairs aloud to a parent or partner, connected by the word "so." There is one extra effect.

CAUSE

1. Peter Zenger accused the governor of New York of being dishonest,

2. Robert Jenkins was smuggling slaves in Spanish territory,

3. Captain Lawrence Washington fought under an English admiral, Edward Vernon,

4. American colonists were British subjects,

5. The English were angry about Jenkins' ear,

EFFECT

a. SO he named his plantation house Mount Vernon.

b. SO the colonies fought on the side of Britain in the War of Jenkins Ear.

c. SO Britain went to war with Spain.

d. SO Zenger was charged with libel and sent to jail.

e. SO the Spanish cut off his ear.

f. SO Zenger was declared not guilty.

WRITING

An editorial is an article that expresses an opinion. With a parent or partner, find an editorial in a local newspaper. Then, in your history journal, write an editorial about Peter Zenger and his libel trial. You may use one of the following first lines: "Newspapers should be free to print the truth." "If government officials are dishonest, citizens have the right to know."

CHAPTER 3

FRENCHMEN AND INDIANS

SUMMARY In 1754, British and French rivalries in North America led to the French and Indian War.

ACCESS

The French and English both had colonies in North American in the early 1700s. New France (Canada) was both similar to and different from the English colonies. Draw a two-circle Venn diagram in your history journal. Label one circle "French Colonies." Label the other "English colonies." List the differences between them in the areas that do not overlap. Write any similarities in the shaded area where the two circles connect.

WORD BANK   camouflage   volley   territory   musket   pelt   surveyor

Choose words from the word bank to complete the sentences. One word is not used at all.

1. An old-fashioned gun is called a _____.

2. The French wanted to expand their _____ in North America.

3. The soldiers wore green and brown uniforms to _____ themselves in the woods.

4. The British gentleman wore a hat made from a beaver _____.

5. Someone who measures and maps land is known as a_____.

CRITICAL THINKING

SEQUENCE OF EVENTS The sentences below list events at the beginning of the French and Indian War. Use numbers to put them in the correct order (use "1" for the first event, and so on.)

___ French and Indians ambush English troops in the wilderness.

___ George Washington carries a message from the governor of Virginia to the French at Fort Dusquesne.

___ The French and English both claimed territory around the Great Lakes and the Ohio River Valley.

___ George Washington and 150 men attack a French scouting party and the French and Indian War begins.

___ The French build forts in the Ohio River Valley.

___ General Braddock dies from a shot in the lungs at the Battle of Fort Duquesne.

___ George Washington loses to the French at Fort Necessity.

WORKING WITH PRIMARY SOURCES

The personal servant of a British officer kept a diary of his experiences during Braddock's march through the wilderness. Here he writes about the moment the British were ambushed:

> So we began our march again, beating the Grenadiers March all the way, never ceasing. There never was an army in the world in more spirits than we were, thinking of reaching Fort Duquesne the day following . . .But we had not got above a mile and a half before three of our guides in the front of me . . . spied the Indians laid down before us. He immediately discharged his piece [gun], turned round his horse [and] cried, the Indians was upon us.

Making Inferences

1. The Grenadiers March is a flute and drum marching tune. Why do you think the British played music on their march?

_____

2. Do you think that music was a good idea?

_____

3. A situation is ironic if it results in an outcome that is different than the one expected. Underline an example of irony in this entry.

_____

CHAPTER 4

A MOST REMARKABLE MAN

SUMMARY William Johnson was an extraordinary colonial leader. He was a soldier, a businessman, and a friend of Indians. He helped lead British and Indian troops to victory against the French in the Battle of Lake George.

ACCESS

Do you have a nickname? Do some family members and friends call you by different names? Three people in this chapter had both a British name and an Indian name. Their Indian names all said something about them. If you could have an Indian name, what would it tell other people about your character? Write your thoughts in your history journal.

WORD BANK   sachem   baronet   confederation   feudal lord

Choose from the word bank to complete the sentences. One word is not used at all.

1. When Johnson was knighted by King, he became an English noble called a _____.

2. Iroquois _____ were the leaders of their tribes.

3. In the Middle Ages in Europe, a _____ ruled over a great estate.

WORD PLAY Look up the word you did not use in the dictionary. Use that word in a sentence in your history journal.

CRITICAL THINKING

FACT OR OPINION A fact is a statement that can be proven. An opinion judges things or people, but it cannot be proved or disproved. Make a two-column chart in your journal. Label one column "Fact" and the other column "Opinion." Write each sentence below from the chapter in the column where it belongs.

1. "' Sir William was a well adjusted European man . . .'"

2. He (Johnson) was named Superintendent of Indian Affairs for the northern colonies."

3. "Molly was said to be 'handsome' and 'uncommonly agreeable'"

4. "Warraghiyagey had hazel eyes and spoke Mohawk with the brogue of an Irishman"

5. Johnson "owned more than 30 trading posts, from Detroit to Albany."

6. "He (Johnson) is a . . .gentleman of uncommon smart sense and even temper.'"

7. Sir William Warraghiyagey Johnson had a zest for life.

8. "Her (Degonwadonti's) grandfather was another of the four Indian kings who had been to London to meet the queen."

WORKING WITH PRIMARY SOURCES

Look at the famous cartoon by Ben Franklin on page 250. He published it in his newspaper, The Pennsylvania Gazette. The whole snake stands for all the American colonies. Each segment stands for a region or a single colony.

1. Start at the head. What does each abbreviation mean?

_____

_____

_____

2. The abbreviation "N.E." stands for which colonies?

_____

3. Two colonies are missing from Franklin's snake. Which are they?

_____

4. Do you think the snake is a good image to represent the colonies? Why or why not?

_____

5. What other images could Franklin have used? Think up a design for your own "Join or Die" cartoon and draw it in your history journal.

_____

PITT STEPS IN
AU REVOIR (GOODBYE), FRANCE

SUMMARY The British won the French and Indian War with the help of their Iroquois allies. England then controlled territory from the Atlantic Ocean to the Mississippi River. Their allies the Iroquois were not rewarded, however, and soon settlers began pushing into Iroquois lands.

ACCESS

Do you think the "French and Indian War" was fought between just the French and the Indians? Create a K-W-L chart like the one on page 8. In the first column, write everything you know about the war. In the second column, write down what you still want to find out. After you finish this chapter, write notes in the final column, " What I Learned."

WORD BANK   provincial   foreign secretary   siege   diplomat

Choose from the word bank to complete the sentences. One word is not used at all.

Sir William Pitt, the British_____, was determined to win the war. He ordered General Jeffrey Amherst to capture the French fort on the St. Lawrence River. Amherst surrounded the fort and laid _____to it. Then, Sir William Johnson took the French fort on the Niagara River. Even though Johnson was a great military leader, Amherst still thought he was _____ and uncivilized.

COMPREHENSION

Put sentences in order, starting with "1".

_____Johnson and Hendrick beat the French at the battle of Lake George

_____General Amherst takes Louisbourg on the St. Lawrence River.

_____General Wolfe dies at the battle of Quebec.

_____The Treaty of Paris ends the war in 1763.

_____The British climb the Heights of Abraham above Quebec.

_____Johnson and his Iroquois allies capture Fort Niagara.

In your history journal, combine these events and the events you put in order in Chapter 3. Make a Sequence of Events chart for the French and Indian War like the one found in Chapter 3.

WRITING

Imagine you are an English reporter at the battle of Quebec. In your history journal, write a headline for your paper. Now imagine you are a French reporter. Write a headline for a French newspaper. How is it different from the headline by the English reporter?

STAYING IN CHARGE
WHAT IS AN AMERICAN?

SUMMARY England tried to prevent American colonists from settling west of the Appalachian Mountains. But pioneers like Daniel Boone ignored the Proclamation of 1763 and kept pushing westward. Immigrant Hector St. John Crèvecoeur wrote a book celebrating the new "Americans" and praising the opportunities that America had to offer.

ACCESS

Have you ever had a friend who made you a promise and went back on his or her word? The English colonies signed many treaties with the Indians and usually broke them. The biggest problem was that both Indians and settlers wanted the same territory. In your history journal, copy a two-circle Venn diagram from page 9. In one circle, write down reasons that Indians wanted territory west of the Appalachian Mountains. In the other circle, write down reasons that settlers wanted this land. Where the circles intersect, write down reasons that the Indians and the settlers shared.

WORD BANK   Great Awakening   pioneer   yeoman farmer   accelerate   scaffold   posterity

Write the correct word next to its definition. One word is not used.

1. _____ future generations

2. _____ religious revival in the 1700s

3. _____ people who own small farms

4. _____ to speed up

5. _____ a supporting framework of poles

CRITICAL THINKING

COMPARE AND CONTRAST These phrases describe ways in which Hector St. John Crèvecoeur thought America and Europe differed in the 1700s. Sort the phrases into two columns, "Europe" and "America," in your history journal.

    Aristocrats own most of land

    People marry others of similar background and social class

    Religion is determined by the state

    People are free to criticize their rulers

    People are yeoman farmers

    Peasants work for the nobility

    People marry others of different national and religious backgrounds

    People work for themselves

    People choose their own religion

    Newspapers and books are censored

WORKING WITH PRIMARY SOURCES

Hector St. John Crèvecoeur said,

> We have no princes, for whom we toil, starve, and bleed. We are the most perfect society now existing in the world.

1. Who are the "princes" Crèvecoeur is talking about?

   _____

2. Do you think America is a "perfect" society? Explain your reasons for saying yes or no in your

   history journal.

A GIRL WHO ALWAYS DID HER BEST

SUMMARY In an era when women's lives centered around home and children, Eliza Lucas Pinckney was also an outstanding businesswoman.

ACCESS

Eliza Lucas Pinckney was an exceptional woman in many ways. In your history journal, copy the main idea map graphic organizer from page 8. In the largest circle put Eliza Lucas's name. In the smaller circles write facts that you learn about her as you read the chapter.

WORD BANK   planters   ginger   indigo   cotton

Use words from the word bank to fill in the paragraph below.

Southern _____ were always looking for new crops to grow and sell. On her father's

plantations, Eliza Lucas experimented with growing _____ and _____, used to make

cloth, and _____, an important spice. Her greatest success came with _____, used to

make blue dye. Twenty years later, South Carolina was exporting more than a million pounds of the

dye. Eliza Lucas Pinckney was so well respected that George Washington was a pallbearer at her

funeral in 1793.

CRITICAL THINKING

Colonial women had some rights but were limited in their choice of activities and professions. Put a "C" next to roles you think women could play in the English colonies, and an "A" next to those they can play in America today.

_____ wife and mother   _____ tavern owner   _____ lawyer

_____ hostess   _____ politician   _____ judge

_____ soldier   _____ shopkeeper   _____ farmer

_____ professor   _____ poet   _____ indentured servant

_____ minister   _____ slave   _____ teacher

Why do you think some roles were possible but others were not? Write your thoughts in your history journal.

WRITING

Imagine that you are a colonial woman writing in her diary. Decide whether you are living in a town, on a small country farm, or on a big plantation. Then, in your history journal, write a diary entry describing one day in your life.

THE RIGHTS OF ENGLISHMEN
A TAXING KING

SUMMARY The rights of Englishmen (and American colonists) come originally from a document called the Magna Carta, signed by King John in 1215. In later centuries, these rights were expanded. When the British imposed taxes on the American colonies, colonists refused to pay them. "No taxation without representation," they cried.

ACCESS

Nearly everybody pays taxes. Taxes pay for government services. Ask a parent or family member what kind of taxes your family pays. Some possibilities are sales tax, property tax, income tax, and inheritance tax. Then copy the main idea map from page 8 in your history journal. In the central circle write the word "taxes." In the smaller circles, write the names of different taxes, and describe what they are.

WORD BANK   Magna Carta   constitution   Bill of Rights   habeas corpus
Glorious Revolution   writ   repeal

Choose from the word bank to complete the sentences. One word is not used at all.

1. English barons forced King John to sign a document in Latin called the _____,

   granting certain rights to lords and wealthy landowners.

2. Anyone who is arrested has the right to ask for a _____ of _____.

3. During England's _____ of 1688, King William and Queen Mary signed a

   _____ that made Parliament more powerful than the monarchy.

4. Parliament decided to _____ the Stamp Tax because the colonists

   demonstrated against it.

WORD PLAY "Magna" is the Latin word for "great, or very large." In five minutes, with a parent or partner make a list of all the words you can think that begin with "magna" or "magni-." Compare lists and look up unfamiliar words in the dictionary.

CRITICAL THINKING

CAUSE AND EFFECT Match the effect in the left column with the correct cause in the right column. Write them as sentences connected with "because." There is one extra cause.

EFFECT

1. Colonists disguised an Indians threw 342 chests of tea into Boston harbor.

2. Parliament passed the Stamp Tax.

3. Colonists refused to buy English goods.

4. England closed the port of Boston.

5. The American colonies banded together to help Boston.

6. Parliament repealed the Stamp Tax.

7. Americans began to talk of independence.

CAUSE

a. Charles Townshend decided to tax glass, paper, lead, paint, and tea.

b. King George was angry about the Boston Tea Party.

c. Boston was on the verge of starvation and ruin.

d. Parliament refused to repeal the tax on tea.

e. they didn't want to be unfairly taxed by England.

f. King George hated the American colonies.

g. they needed money to help pass for the French and Indian War.

d. colonists attacked British stamp agents.

_____because_____

WRITE ABOUT IT Imagine that you are visiting Boston from a distant town and you witness the Boston Tea Party. In your history journal, write a letter to a friend describing the scene on the Boston docks on the night of December 16. 1773. Add as many details as you can think of from the reading.

CHAPTER 12

THE FIREBRANDS

SUMMARY Three men, Sam Adams, Patrick Henry, and Thomas Paine, helped spark the American Revolution.

12 The Firebrands

ACCESS

Can you name the leaders in your school? What leadership qualities do they have? Copy the main idea graphic organizer from page 8 . In the central circle, write the words "Leader." In the smaller circles, write words that describe a great leader. Match each quality with a person you have read about in From Colonies to Country.

WORD BANK   firebrand   demean   committees of correspondence   Sons of Liberty   ominous

Choose from the word bank to complete the sentences. One word is not used at all.

1. The young _____ inspired the audience with his impassioned speeches.

2. _____communicated with each other throughout the American

   colonies.

3. Sam Adams and the _____ led the fight against the Stamp Act.

4. The _____ gray clouds warned us that a storm was coming.

CRITICAL THINKING

COMPARE AND CONTRAST The sentences below describe the actions of Sam Adams, Patrick Henry, and Thomas Paine. In your history journal, copy the model of the three-circle Venn diagram below. Label each circle with one person's name. Now copy the phrases below in the correct circles. The phrases that apply to only one character go in that person's circle. The phrases that describe the actions of two people go in the area where the two circles belonging to those two characters connect. Any actions of all three belong in the shaded area formed by all three circles.

organized the Sons of Liberty   wrote Common Sense

started the Committees of Correspondence   came from England

was a good speaker   lived in Virginia

served in the House of Burgesses   was a failure in business

said "Give me liberty or give me death"   enlisted in Continental army

wanted independence from England   lived in Boston

wrote "These are the times that try men's souls" was a good writer

Three-Circle Venn
Diagram

WORKING WITH PRIMARY SOURCES:

Read the passage from *Common Sense* by Thomas Paine.

In the following pages I offer nothing more than simple facts, plain argument, and common sense. . . .

I have heard it asserted by some that, as America has flourished under her former connection with Great Britain, the same connection is necessary towards her future happiness, and will always have the same effect. Nothing can be more fallacious than this kind of argument. We may as well assert that, because a child has thrived upon milk, it is never to have meat."

1. Paine calls his words "simple" and "plain." Why does he emphasize the clearness of his argument?

_____

2. To whom do you think Paine is speaking?

_____

3. To what does Paine compare the young American colonies? Underline the comparison.

_____

4. Look up the word "fallacious" in the dictionary. Use the word in a sentence.

_____

CHAPTER 13

A MASSACRE IN BOSTON

SUMMARY In March 1770, a clash between British soldiers and a Boston mob fueled the colonists' anger against England.

ACCESS

Two people who witness the same event often cannot agree on what really happened. With a parent or a family member, discuss an episode in your own life. Do you both remember it the same way? Think about why memories might be different. Write your thoughts in your history journal.

WORD BANK   redcoats   Quartering Act   massacre   propaganda   militia   deserters

Choose words from the word bank to complete the sentences. One word is not used at all.

1. Bostonians disliked the British law called the _____. It ordered colonists to house

   British soldiers in their own homes.

2. Colonists called British soldiers _____ because of the color of their uniforms.

3. The First Continental Congress suggested that each colony form its own _____ to defend

   from British attack.

4. Sam Adams used _____ to convince colonists that the clash between British

   soldiers and a Boston mob was really a _____.

WORD PLAY Look up in the dictionary the word you did not use. Write your own sentence to include the word.

CRITICAL THINKING

Review the events leading up to the Revolutionary War in Chapters 11 and 13. Match the dates on the left with the events on the right. Then make a timeline like the one on p. 9 from the dates and events in your history journal.

1765	The First Continental Congress
1767	The Boston Tea Party
1770	The Boston Massacre
1773	The Stamp Tax
1774	The Townshend Acts

WORKING WITH PRIMARY SOURCES

Lawyer John Adams argued that in the Boston Massacre, British soldiers such as one named Montgomery fired their muskets in self-defense. To the jury Adams described the scene outside the Customs House on the night of March 5, 1770:

> When the multitude was shouting and hazzaing, and threatening life, the bells ringing, the mob whistling, screaming and rending an Indian yell; the people from all quarters throwing every species of rubbish they could pick up in the street . . . Montgomery in particular smote with a club and knocked down . . . what could he do? It is impossible you should find him guilty of murder.

Circle the correct answers.

1. When Adams asks, "What could he do?" he is suggesting that:

   a. Montgomery had no right to fight back.

   b. It was natural for Montgomery to try to defend himself.

   c. Montgomery should have stayed on the ground until the fight was over.

2. Adams suggests that the jury should not find Montgomery guilty of murder because

   a. Only a British jury has the right to try a British soldier.

   b. Self-defense is not murder.

   c. No one was killed that night.

CHAPTER 14

ONE IF BY LAND, TWO IF BY SEA

SUMMARY The Revolutionary War begins at the Battle of Lexington on April 19, 1776.

ACCESS

Because brave Americans risked their lives in Boston more than 200 years ago, we are a free country today. As you read the chapter, write down a few sentences about what each person had to do with the first battle of the Revolution.

Paul Revere

_____

_____

Billy Dawes

_____

_____

William Dawes

_____

_____

Dr. Samuel Prescott

_____

_____

Mother Batherick

_____

_____

Bonus: What poet wrote about the battle?

_____

_____

WORD BANK   Patriot   Loyalist   minutemen

Find the definitions of these words on pp. 69 and 73. Then write a sentence in which you use all three of the words.

CRITICAL THINKING

SEQUENCE OF EVENTS The sentences below describe the sequence of events leading up to the Battles of Lexington and Concord. Use numbers to put the events in their proper order.

_____ The minutemen beat the British at Concord.

_____ A signal was lit in the tower of Old North Church.

_____ The minutemen grabbed their weapons.

_____ Paul Revere and Billy Dawes rode through the countryside, warning "The British are coming!"

_____ Colonists stockpiled cannonballs and gunpowder in Concord, Massachusetts.

_____ The first shot of the Revolutionary War was fired at Lexington.

_____ The British decided to march on Concord.

WRITING Find Henry Wadsworth Longfellow's "The Midnight Ride of Paul Revere" in a book or online. With a parent or partner, take turns reading the poem out loud. Then create a comic book of the events in the poem. For each stanza, draw one boxed picture, or "panel." Write one or two important lines from the stanza above each panel.

CHAPTER 15

AN AMERICAN ORIGINAL

SUMMARY A tough frontiersman named Ethan Allan made a daring raid on British-held Fort Ticonderoga and captured it for the Patriots.

ACCESS

Ethan Allan was a man who played many roles. Copy the main idea map from page 8. In the largest box write Ethan Allan's name. In each of the smaller boxes write one fact you learn about him as you read the chapter.

WORD BANK   Enlightenment   Jehovah   sinewy   catamounts   predators

Choose words from the word bank to complete the sentences. One word is not used at all.

1. _____ is a Hebrew word for God.

2. During the _____, European thinkers made great advances in scientific knowledge and political philosophy.

3. Cougars, pumas, and panthers are all types of big cats called _____.

4. Large _____ such as wolves and mountain lions hunt smaller mammals and birds for food.

Look up the word you did not use in the dictionary. Which meaning of the word applies in the description of Ethan Allan on p. 76?

_____

CRITICAL THINKING

COMPARE AND CONTRAST Ethan Allen and Benedict Arnold were very different men, but they were similar in some ways. In your history journal, use a Venn diagram to list words describing each man. Descriptions for both should go in the middle of your diagram.

Was a traitor	Wore a formal uniform
Was a good fighter	Wore frontier clothes
Was a Continental officer	Used rough language
Was a loyal patriot	Had a personal servant
Was exceptionally big and strong	Was a good leader

WRITING The title of this chapter is "An American Original." Look up the word "original" in a dictionary. Then, in your history journal, write two paragraphs about why that description applies to Ethan Allen. Use details from the book.

CHAPTER 16

ON THE WAY TO THE CONTINENTAL CONGRESS

SUMMARY In 1775, a group of distinguished colonial leaders met at the Continental Congress in Philadelphia to debate the fate of their country.

ACCESS

The Revolutionary War divided the colonies into two groups of people, Patriots and Loyalists. Draw a two-circle Venn diagram in your history journal. Label one circle "Patriots." Label the other "Loyalists." Write phrases that you think describe Patriots in one circle. Write phrases that apply to Loyalists in another circle. Phrases that apply to both can go in the area where the circles overlap.

WORD BANK   eloquence   Commonwealth   rabble   delegate

Choose words from the Word Bank to complete the sentences. One word is not used at all.

1. In the 21st century, Canada, Australia, and New Zealand are all members of the British _____ of nations.

2. Many in the British Parliament considered colonial Patriots to be a ragged _____ of lawbreakers.

3. Patrick Henry spoke with great _____ about liberty and freedom.

WORD PLAY Two words make up "commonwealth." What do they suggest about the purpose of a commonwealth of nations? In your history journal, write down two other word combinations that you might use to describe a group of nations bound together by allegiance to one ruler.

CRITICAL THINKING

WHO AM I? Use the name bank to identify the people described in the statements below.

Name Bank

    Richard Henry Lee   John Witherspoon   Benjamin Rush

    Benjamin Harrison   Francis Hopkinson   John Hancock

    Philip Livingston   Charles Carroll

1. I was the only Roman Catholic delegate at the continental Congress. _____

2. I set up the first medical clinic in America. _____

3. I was a Presbyterian minister who became president of Princeton College. _____

4. I was an inventor and scientist from New Jersey. _____

5. I was an elegant Virginian with a missing finger. _____

6. My son and great-grandson became president of the United States. _____

7. I was a wealthy New Yorker who believed in political and religious freedom. _____

NAMING A GENERAL

SUMMARY The Continental Congress formed a Continental Army and appointed an extraordinary man to whip the untrained recruits into shape: General George Washington.

ACCESS

You probably already know a lot about George Washington. In your history journal, make a K-W-L chart. In the left-hand column, write what you already know about Washington. In the middle column, write what you what to know. In the right column, write what you learned from this chapter. Add to this chart as you read the next chapters in your history book

WORD BANK

WORD PLAY The word "militia" comes from the Latin word "miles," meaning soldier. Can you think of two more words with the same root?

CRITICAL THINKING

CLASSIFICATION In 1775, Great Britain was the mightiest power in the world. Yet it had both strengths and weaknesses as it began the war against its American colonies. The words below describe both British advantages and disadvantages in the war. Make a two-column chart labeled "British Advantages" and "British Disadvantages." Put the descriptions in the correct column.

Unfamiliar with the terrain   Well-trained professional army

Best navy in world   Fighting against amateur soldiers

Fighting in enemy territory Ruled by a government 3,000 miles away

WORKING WITH PRIMARY SOURCES
READING BETWEEN THE LINES

Reverend William Emerson visited the Continental army camp in Cambridge, Massachusetts, shortly after General Washington arrived to take command. He described the different colonial camps:

> [The camps] are as different in their form as the owners are in their dress; and every tent is a portraiture of the temper and taste of the persons that incamp in it. Some are made of boards, some of sailcloth . . . Others are made of stone and turf, and others again of birch and other brush. Some are thrown up in a hurry. . . . Others are curiously wrought [made] with doors and windows . . . Some are your proper tents . . .and look like the regular camp of the enemy. . . .I think that the great variety of the American camp is, upon the whole, rather a beauty than a blemish to the army.

Answer the questions on the next page in your history journal.

1. To what does Emerson compare the different "form[s]" of the camps?

2. What kind of a person would build his shelter "in a hurry"? What kind of person would build it with "doors and windows"?

3. What does Emerson suggest that the "regular camp of the enemy" looks like? What does the appearance of their camps say about the British army?

4. What does the word "blemish" mean in this passage?

5. Does Emerson have a positive or negative opinion of the Continental army camp? Circle the sentence that reveals his opinion.

THE WAR OF THE HILLS
FIGHTING PALM TREES

SUMMARY The British won a very costly victory against the Patriots at Breed's Hill and Bunker's Hill outside Boston. When a British fleet ran aground in Charleston Harbor, Patriots bombarded them from the shore and the British were forced to retreat.

ACCESS

South Carolina has a palmetto tree on its state flag, in honor of the battle that was fought in Charleston in 1775. The tree is a symbol. Research five other state flags. What meanings do the images on the flags have? Write the results of your research in your history journal.

WORD BANK   palmetto   mortification   provincial   shoals   fortifications   aground

Use the words below to fill in the blanks in the following paragraph.

The British fleet ran _____ on the _____ of Charleston Harbor. British commander Sir Peter Parker decided this was a good opportunity to bomb the fort on Sullivan's Island in the middle of the harbor. But the walls of the _____ were built with sand and soft _____ logs. When the cannonballs hit the walls, the shells sank into the soft wood. To Parker's great _____, the _____ troops of South Carolina had beaten the best navy in the world!

WORD PLAY Look on page 95 to find a definition of "mortification." The word comes from the Latin word for death, "mort." Can you think of a well-known expression that links great humiliation with death? _____

CRITICAL THINKING

CAUSE AND EFFECT Draw a line from each cause and connect it to the result, or effect. Then read the matched pairs aloud to a parent or partner.

Cause

1. The Americans opened fire when the enemy was almost on top of the hill

2. Massachusetts soldiers built defenses on Breed's Hill

3. The British ships were grounded on sandbars in Charleston harbor

4. The Massachusetts troops ran out of gunpowder

5. The British shells stuck in the sides of the fort in the harbor

Effect

1. SO the British weren't able to destroy the fort.

2. SO the British captured Breed's Hill and Bunker Hill.

3. SO the South Carolina troops bombarded the ships from the shore.

4. SO the British decided to attack the hill.

5. SO they hit the British with great accuracy.

WORKING WITH PRIMARY SOURCES

Abigail Adams could hear the Battle of Bunker Hill from her home in Braintree, just south of Boston. She wrote to her husband John in Philadelphia:

> The day; perhaps the decisive day is come on which the fate of America depends. . . . Charlestown is laid in ashes. The battle began upon our intrenchments upon Bunkers Hill, a Saturday morning about 3 o clock and has not ceased yet and tis now 3 o'clock Sabbath afternoon. . . .How many have fallen we know not--the constant roar of the cannon is so distressing that we can not eat, drink, or sleep.

1. Why does Abigail think that the battle may be important?

2. How many hours had the battle raged when Abigail wrote this letter?

3. How does the noise of the cannon make Abigail feel?

   a. worried   b. happy   c. sleepy

CHAPTER 20

DECLARING INDEPENDENCE

SUMMARY The Declaration of Independence cut the colonies' ties with Britain and announced to the world that the new United States of America was founded on principles of liberty and equality.

ACCESS

The authors of the Declaration of Independence wrote that "all men are created equal." Yet everyone has differing abilities and talents. So what do these famous words really mean? In your history journal, copy the main idea map from page 8. In the largest circle put the words "All men are created equal." In each of the smaller circles, write one way in which all people in the world can be considered equal.

WORD BANK   declaration   antislavery   compromise

Fill in the blanks with the words below.

To be against the ownership of one human being by another is to be _____.

A _____ is an announcement or a statement of intent.

To _____ is to agree after each side has given up claims or demands.

WORD PLAY With a Parent or Partner

The prefix "anti" comes from the Greek root meaning "against." With a parent or partner, in five minutes write down all the words you can think of that start with "anti." Then look the words up in a dictionary to see if they are listed.

CRITICAL THINKING

Contemporaries Thomas Jefferson and Benjamin Banneker shared many of the same interests but lived very different lives. In your history journal, copy the Venn diagram from page 35. Label one circle "Thomas Jefferson" and the other circle "Benjamin Banneker." List the differences between them in the areas that do not overlap. Write any similarities in the shaded area where the two circles connect.

Grew up on a plantation

Played the violin

Lived in Maryland

Wrote the Declaration of Independence

Lived in Virginia

Was a black man

Was a white man

Was an Enlightenment thinker

Grew up on a small tobacco farm

Was a great reader

Wrote an almanac

WORKING WITH PRIMARY SOURCES

IN YOUR OWN WORDS The following passage is part of the final paragraph of the Declaration of Independence. In your history journal, rewrite this passage in your own words. (Work with a parent or partner if you can.)

> We . . . do, in the name and by the authority of the good people of these colonies, solemnly publish and declare, that these united colonies are, and of right ought to be, free and independent states: that they are absolved from all allegiance to the British Crown, and that all political connections between them and the state of Great Britain is, and ought to be, totally dissolved.

1. Use a dictionary to define the word "absolved": _____

2 Use a dictionary to define the word "allegiance":_____

3. Why do you think the authors wrote that the "united colonies" are "free and independent states" rather than a "free and independent nation"?

CHAPTER 21 SIGNING UP

SUMMARY Signing the Declaration of Independence was a bold and courageous act.

ACCESS

What were the risks in signing signing the Declaration of Independence? What was at least one big benefit of signing the document that started the Revolutionary War? As you read the chapter, write your thoughts in your history journal.

WORD BANK   forfeit   pensive   dissenting   gilded   transient

Find the following words in your book. Then write them next to their definitions below.

1. thoughtful _____

2. covered with a thin layer of gold _____

3. to lose because of some error or crime _____

4. lasting only a short time _____

5. differing _____

CRITICAL THINKING

WORKING WITH PRIMARY SOURCES In his journal, Isaac Bangs described the scene in New York the day after the Declaration of Independence was read:

> Last night the statue on the Bowling Green representing . . . George Rex . . . was pulled down by the populace. In it were 4,000 pounds of lead . . . both man and horse were covered with gold leaf. The lead . . .is to be run up into musket balls for the use of the Yankees, when it is hoped that the [products] of the leaden George will make as deep impressions in the bodies of some of his red coated and Tory subjects.

Answer the questions in your history journal.

1. Rex is the Latin word for king. Who is George Rex?

2. What two materials is the statue made of? Which will probably be more useful to the Patriots? Why?

3. When Bangs says he hopes that "the leaden George will make deep impressions in the bodies of his red coated subjects" he means

    a. ___ he hopes the king will be good to the Yankees.

    b. ___ he hopes the king will impress his subjects.

    c. ___ he hopes the lead musket balls will wound British soldiers.

4. Do you think Bangs is a Patriot or a Tory? Explain your reasons.

REVOLUTIONARY WOMEN AND CHILDREN

SUMMARY Women's contribution to winning the Revolutionary War was vital on both the home front and the battlefront.

ACCESS

Women's roles in society have changed a lot since the 1700s. For instance, today women can join most branches of the military. Back then they were not allowed to enlist in the army. Some did anyway. As you read the chapter, complete the chart below by checking the boxes that apply to these "Founding Mothers of the Revolution."

	Soldier	Writer	Manager of Farm and Home
Abigail Adams			
Molly Brant			
Anna Marie Lane			
Eliza Pinckney			
Deborah Sampson			
Mercy Otis Warren			
Phillis Wheatley			
Eliza Wilkinson			

WORD BANK   foment   iniquitous   scheme   prosperity

Choose words from the Word Bank to complete the sentences. One word is not used at all.

1. His illegal _____for making money landed him in jail.

2. Samuel Adams was determined to _____ a revolution.

3. Slavery is one of the oldest and most _____ of human crimes.

WORD PLAY In a dictionary, look up the word you did not use and write out its definition. What shorter word does it include?

WORKING WITH PRIMARY SOURCES

In 1775, African American slave Phillis Wheatley wrote a poem dedicated "To His Excellency General Washington" and sent it to Washington himself. The poem's last four lines read:

> Proceed, great chief, with virtue on thy side,
> Thy ev'ry action let the goddess [Columbia] guide,
> A crown, a mansion, and a throne that shine,
> With gold unfading, WASHINGTON! Be thine.

Write your answers in your history journal. Work with a parent or partner if you can.

1. "Columbia" is a poetic term for "America." According to Wheatley, what should Columbia guide?

2. What does the poem say Washington deserves as a reward for service to his country?

Washington answered Wheatley's letter:

Miss Phillis . . . I thank you most sincerely for your polite notice of me in the elegant lines you enclosed . . . If you should ever come to Cambridge, or near headquarters, I shall be happy to see a person so favored by the Muses, . . . I am with great respect, your obedient and humble servant.

1. Why do you think Washington calls her "Miss Phillis" instead of "Miss Wheatley"?

2. What are the "Muses"? Look the term up in an encyclopedia and write down the definition.

3. Which Muse do you think Washington was referring to?

4. In the 18th century, "I am your obedient and humble servant" was a common complimentary close to a letter. What close might Washington choose today?

FREEDOM FIGHTERS

SUMMARY James Forten and other patriotic African Americans wanted to fight for freedom in the American Revolution. More than other Americans, they understood what "all men are created equal" truly meant.

ACCESS

What role did black men and women—free and enslaved—play in the rebellion? In your history journal, copy the K-W-L Chart from page 8. In the first column, write everything you know about blacks in the American Revolution. In the second column, write down what you still want to find out. As you read through the next few chapters, write notes in the final column, " What I Learned."

WORD BANK   privateer   powder boys   renounce   pueblo

Choose words from the Word Bank to complete the sentences.

1. American_____ roamed the coast of North America, searching for British ships to attack.

2. Explorers Francisco Dominguez and Silvestre Velez de Escalante discovered an old Indian village called a _____ in Utah.

3. James Forten swore that he would never _____ his country.

4. During sea battles, daring _____ kept the ships' cannon supplied with gunpowder.

CRITICAL THINKING

MAIN IDEA AND SUPPORTING IDEAS Each sentence in italics below states a main idea from the chapter. Put a check mark in the blanks in front of all the sentences that support or tell more about the main idea.

James Forten believed that the words "all men are created equal" were worth fighting for.

____ a. When he was captured by the British, Forten went to prison rather than be a traitor to his country.

____ b. Forten was a wealthy and successful sail maker in Philadelphia.

____ c. At fourteen, Forten became a powder monkey on an American privateer.

____ d. Forten helped found an antislavery society.

The world of the 18th century was like a ladder, where everyone had a particular rung to stand on.

____ a. Most people did not really understand what "all men are created equal" meant.

____ b. The Continental army accepted black soldiers in 1778.

____ c. The new idea that people all have equal rights seemed wild and radical.

SOLDIERS FROM EVERYWHERE
BLACK SOLDIERS

SUMMARY Attracted by the ideal of liberty, men of many different nationalities made important contributions to the Revolution. When Lord Dunmore promised freedom to anyone who became a British soldier, black Virginians were faced with a difficult decision.

ACCESS

Pretend you are an enslaved man living in Virginia when Lord Dunmore offers freedom to any slave who fights for the British. What will you do? Make a two-column chart in your history journal. List the benefits of accepting the offer on one side. List the possible drawbacks, such as putting your life in danger, on the other side.

WORD BANK   marquis   drillmaster   recruits   imperious   emblazoned

1. To be haughty and commanding is to be _____.

2. A _____ is a kind of French nobleman.

3. Young men who have recently enlisted in the army are called _____.

4. _____ means inscribed on a surface.

5. A _____ trains soldiers to march, follow orders, and use weapons.

CRITICAL THINKING

COMPARE AND CONTRAST   The sentences below describe the Marquis de Lafayette, Baron Friedrich von Steuban, and Haym Salomon. Look at the model of a three-circle Venn diagram below. Copy a larger version in your history journal. One circle is for each of these people. Place the phrases below in the correct circles. The phrases that apply to only one character go in that person's circle. The phrases that describe actions of two people go in the area where the two circles belonging to those two characters connect. Any actions of all three belong in the circle area formed by all three circles.

came from Poland	was Jewish
was a drillmaster	came from Prussia
came from France	helped the Americans
was a businessman	lent money to Congress
fought for the Patriots	believed in liberty
was rich and noble	was a professional soldier
was friends with Washington	had a roaring voice

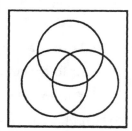

Three-circle Venn diagram

FIGHTING A WAR; *HOWE* BILLY WISHED
FRANCE WOULDN'T JOIN IN

SUMMARY Washington's untrained, ill-prepared army lost its first big battle with the British at Long Island. But soon the Continental army was to win three surprise victories at Trenton, Princeton, and most important, Saratoga.

ACCESS

In your history journal, make a timeline, like the one on page 9, for Battles of the American Revolution. On the date line, write the dates 1775, 1776, 1777, 1778, 1779, 1780, 1781, 1782, and 1783. Then write the following battles in the boxes to the right when they happened: Lexington and Concord; Bunker Hill; Sullivan's Island; Great Bridge; Long Island; Trenton; Saratoga.

WORD BANK   guerilla   sniped   mercenaries   retreat

Choose words from the Word Bank to complete the sentence below. One word is not used at all.

The _____ fighters hidden behind the trees _____ at the Hessian _____ marching along the main path.

Find the word you did not use on page 124 of your textbook. What does the word mean in this sentence?_____

CRITICAL THINKING

CAUSE AND EFFECT Draw a line between in the left column and the correct cause in the right column. In your history journal, write them as sentences connected with "because." There is one extra cause.

Effect

1. General Burgoyne decided to capture the Hudson River Valley

2. The French joined the war on the American side

3. General Washington won the battle of Trenton

4. General Howe did not pursue Washington into Pennsylvania

5. Burgoyne's army took two months to march from Fort Ticonderoga to Saratoga

6. The Americans beat the British at Saratoga

Cause

a. He surprised Hessian troops who were celebrating Christmas.

b. American sharpshooters were deadly accurate in their aim.

c. Howe did not like to fight in cold weather.

d. Burgoyne recaptured Fort Ticonderoga.

e. Patriots blocked the road and ambushed British soldiers.

f. He wanted to cut New England off from the other colonies.

g. The French heard about the American victory at Saratoga.

WORKING WITH PRIMARY SOURCES

READING BETWEEN THE LINES Before the Battle of Brandywine in July 1777, British major Patrick Fergusson was on a scouting expedition close to enemy lines. He saw two officers of the Continental army on horseback:

> I ordered three good shots to steal near . . .and fire at them, but the idea disgusted me. I recalled the order. [The man with a cocked hat passed] within a hundred yards of us, upon which I advanced from the woods towards him. On my calling he stopped, but after looking at me, proceeded. . . . As I was within that distance at which . . . I could have lodged half-a-dozen of balls in or about him before he was out of my reach, I had only to determine. But it was not pleasant to fire at the back of an unoffending individual, who was [doing] . . . his duty, so I left him alone.

Answer the questions in your history journal.

1. Why does Fergusson take back his order to shoot the American officers?

2. How would you characterize the man in the cocked hat?

    a. brave

    b. cowardly

    c. stupid

1. Fergusson says that it was "not pleasant" to shoot someone in the back. What do you think he means?

    a. It was not honorable.

    b. It was not safe.

    c. It would not be approved by his superiors.

A day later, Fergusson discovered that the man with the cocked hat was actually General George Washington! He wrote, "I am not sorry that I did not know at the time who it was." If Fergusson had known his identity, do you think he would have shot Washington? Why or why not?

VALLEY FORGE TO VINCENNES

SUMMARY From their difficult winter at Valley Forge, the Continental Army emerged as a fighting force to be reckoned with. Meanwhile, in the west, a daring frontiersman named George Rogers Clark forced the British from the Ohio River Valley.

ACCESS

George Rogers Clark was a larger-than-life character who accomplished amazing things. In your history journal, copy the main idea map graphic organizer from page 8. In the largest circle put Clark's name. In the smaller circles write facts that you learn about him as you read the chapter.

WORD BANK   mutiny   quartermaster   serfs

Choose words from the Word Bank to complete the sentences below.

1. Thaddeus Kosciuszko freed his _____ when he returned to Poland,

1. Nathanael Greene, the _____ of the army, was in charge of obtaining supplies.

2. Conditions at Valley Forge were so desperate that officers feared the soldiers might stage a

   _____.

WORD PLAY "Serf" comes from the Latin word "servus," or slave. Other common English words are derived from the same root. How many can you name? Write them in your history journal.

CRITICAL THINKING

FACT OR OPINION A fact is a statement that can be proven. An opinion judges things or people, but it cannot be proved or disproved. Make a two-column chart in your journal. Label one column "Fact" and the other column "Opinion." Write each sentence below from the chapter in the column where it belongs.

1. "They [the army] became a team: strong, confident, and proud of themselves."
2. "Disease swept the camp."
3. "[Valley Forge] had been named for a nearby iron foundry."
4. "Greene brought enormous energy and determination to everything he did."
5. "[Von Steuben] seemed to thrive on hard work, and nothing upset him."
6. "Clark was a frontiersman and a Patriot, as well as an Indian fighter."
7. "Clark was smart; he was also brave and daring."
8. "[Von Steuben] made all the officers set their watches by the same clock."

WORKING WITH PRIMARY SOURCES

Seventeen-year-old Continental soldier Joseph Plumb Martin remembered the hard march to Valley Forge:

> The army was now not only starved but naked. . . . I procured a small piece of raw cowhide and made myself a pair of moccasins, which kept my feet (while they lasted) from the frozen ground. . . . The only alternative I had was to . . , go barefoot, as hundreds of my companions had to, till they might be tracked by their blood upon the rough frozen ground.

WRITING Imagine that you are a teenage soldier in the Continental Army. In your history journal, write a letter to your family describing your experiences during the winter of 1777–1778. What will you tell them? What might you leave out? How do you want your family to react when they read your letter?

THE STATES WRITE CONSTITUTIONS

SUMMARY Lawmakers who wrote state constitutions during the war wrestled with issues of individual rights and balance of power within state governments.

ACCESS

Pretend that you are a state leader of an imaginary state formed after the American Revolution. Your task is to write a constitution for the state. In your history journal, copy down the main idea map on page 8. In the central circle, write the name of your imaginary state. In the smaller circles, write down the rights that every person in your state will have.

WORD BANK
separation of powers   legislative branch   executive branch   judicial branch

Choose words from the Word Bank to complete the definitions below.

1. The branch of government that decides if the laws are carried out fairly is the

_____.

2. The doctrine that power should be shared equally among different branches of government is called _____.

3. The branch of government that carries out the laws is the _____.

4. The branch of government that makes the laws is the _____.

CRITICAL THINKING

DRAWING CONCLUSIONS Each of the sentences in italics below is taken from the chapter. Write a check mark in front of the conclusions that can be drawn from reading the sentence.

1. *[State leaders] didn't want anything in America like a too-powerful English king or a too-powerful parliament.*

_____a. State leaders distrusted the English king.

_____b. State legislatures were corrupt and dictatorial.

_____c. State leaders wanted power to be divided among many people in state government.

2. *In some states Roman Catholics, Jews, Baptists, and atheists were barred from voting or holding public office.*

_____a. Some states discriminated against people on the basis of their religion.

_____b. Jews and Roman Catholics rebelled against the new state constitutions.

_____c. Many people distrusted people different from themselves.

3. The idea that government should guarantee freedom and equal opportunity in written documents was totally new.

_____a. Citizens of other nations had no rights at all.

_____b. Citizens of all U.S. states would have the same rights.

_____c. The state constitutions were the first documents to guarantee certain freedoms in writing.

WRITING

How have things changed since the Revolution? Read the list in italic type on page 136. Do Americans argue about the same things today? Write a few paragraphs about two issues you think Americans do disagree about today. (Work with a parent or partner if you can.)

CHAPTER 30

MORE ABOUT CHOICES

SUMMARY The decisions Henry Knox, Mary Katherine Goddard, and other Americans made during the Revolution would help mold a way of life for future generations.

ACCESS

Every day we make choices that change our lives in large and small ways. Write about one decision you made that has been important in your life or in the life of a friend or family member.

WORD BANK

contagious   satire   artillery   ironic

Choose words from the Word Bank to complete the definitions below.

1. When Tom Tell-Truth told Americans to obey the British without question, he was being

   _____.

2. The _____ fired on the attacking British troops.

3. _____ is a form of humor that ridicules society using irony and sarcasm.

4. When a disease is easy to catch we say it is _____.

CRITICAL THINKING

SEQUENCE OF EVENTS Mary Katherine Goddard became a printer. This decision caused a series of events in her life. It also had effects on the Revolutionary War. In the sequence of events chart below, write "Became a printer" in the first box. Then fill in the other boxes with other events in her life.

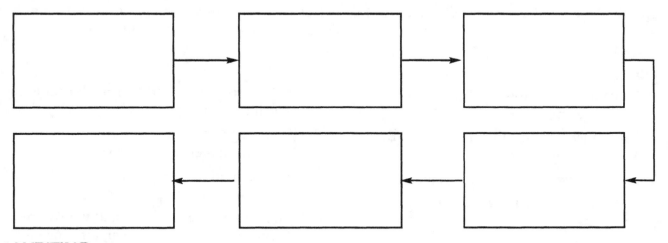

WRITING

Choose either Henry Knox or Mary Katherine Goddard. Pretend you could interview them for a TV news program. What five questions would you ask? Write your questions in your history journal.

WHEN IT'S OVER, SHOUT HOORAY

SUMMARY *A combined force of American and French troops cornered the British at Yorktown and forced General Cornwallis to surrender.*

ACCESS

Go to your timeline for Battles of the American Revolution you made in your history journal. Add the following battles to the boxes on the right of when they happened: Princeton, Brandywine, Vincennes, Camden, Yorktown, and the Treaty of Paris. (If you are uncertain about dates, go to the map in the Atlas section of your book.)

WORD BANK   stalemate   Bay   dashing

Choose words from the Word Bank to complete the sentences below.

1. British and American troops fought each other to a _____ in the North; neither side could win decisively.

2. The handsome young nobleman the Marquis de Lafayette made a _____ figure on the battlefield.

3. The Susquehanna River empties into the Chesapeake _____ , a large body of water that leads to the Atlantic Ocean.

CRITICAL THINKING

CAUSE AND EFFECT Draw a line between the effect in the left column with the correct cause in the right column. Then read the matched pairs aloud to a parent or partner, connected with "because." There is one extra cause.

Effect

1. General Washington decided to march to Yorktown

2. The British thought they had beaten the Patriots in the South

3. General Cornwallis was frustrated

4. Sir William Howe resigned as chief of the British forces

5. The Americans and French won the Battle of Yorktown

6. General Henry Clinton sent the British army south

7. General Cornwallis couldn't receive new men or supplies

Cause

a. The French fleet kept the British fleet from reaching him.

b. He thought the South was full of Loyalists who would help the British.

c. He was tired of being criticized for the British failures in the war.

d. The Marquis de Lafayette and the Baron Steuben met Washington at Yorktown.

e. He found out the French fleet was sailing to Chesapeake Bay.

f. The British won big, important battles at Charleston and Camden, South Carolina.

g. American guerilla fighters kept beating the British in small battles.

They outflanked and outnumbered the British.

_____because_____

ALL OVER THE MAP

Look at the map of the Battle of Yorktown in the Atlas section of your book. Answer the following questions:

1. Which general marched his forces to Yorktown first?_____

2. From what direction did this general approach Yorktown?_____

3. Which generals approached Yorktown from the northwest?

_____

4. What states did George Washington and the Comte de Rochambeau pass through on their way to Yorktown?_____

5. In what direction were they marching? _____

6. How many miles did they travel? (Use the map scale.) _____

7. How did Washington's troops travel from Maryland to Yorktown?

_____

EXPERIMENTING WITH A NATION
LOOKING NORTHWEST

SUMMARY Under the Articles of Confederation, the government was weak. However, it passed the Northwest Ordinance. That provided a way for territories to become states.

ACCESS

Compare the map of The New Nation, 1783, in the Atlas section with the map of the United States on the inside front cover of this guide. What new states would be formed by the purple territory? Trace an outline of the eastern United States up to the Mississippi River and draw in the new states.

WORD BANK   ordinance   Conestoga   involuntary servitude   inflation   township

Choose words from the Word Bank to complete the sentences below. One word is not used at all.

1. People traveled west over the Appalachian Mountains in big _____ wagons.

2. Slavery is a form of _____.

1. Due to the effects of _____, it cost $3 instead of $2 to buy a gallon of milk.

4. A _____ is an area of land composed of a number of smaller towns and villages.

Look up the definition of the word that was not used in a dictionary. Write it in a sentence._____

CRITICAL THINKING

DRAWING CONCLUSIONS Write the letter "S" next to the sentences below that describe a success of the Confederation government. Write "F" next to those sentences that describe a failure.

1. _____ The Confederation Congress passed the Northwest Ordinance in 1787

2. _____ Each state printed its own money.

3. _____ The Northwest Ordinance required that each town set aside land for public schools.

4. _____ The Confederation Congress had no power to collect taxes.

5. _____ The Northwest Ordinance outlawed slavery and indentured servitude in the territories.

6. _____ The states had their own navies.

7. _____ The president of the Confederation government had no power.

USING PRIMARY SOURCES

WRITING People didn't agree about women's education after the Revolution. One school principal said:

> to be much learned is not an essential requirement in a female. The professions are not proper to the sex, it is not looked for in you to be doctresses, teachers of the arts and sciences, politics, or law.

But at another school, girls learned:

> reading and writing in both the German and English languages, also arithmetic, sewing, knitting, and other feminine crafts. . . . history, geography, and music.

In your history journal, write a few paragraphs about how things have changed today for girls in American schools.

CHAPTER 34

A MAN WITH IDEAS

SUMMARY Thomas Jefferson was a many of many talents and the author of some of America's most important documents.

ACCESS

Thomas Jefferson is one of the most important of the Founding Fathers. Imagine you could interview Jefferson. First, skim through the chapter. Then, in your history journal, write down five questions you would ask him. The first might be "What are you most proud of?" Now read the chapter carefully and write the answers to the questions as you imagine Jefferson might answer them.

WORD BANK   decimal system   piedmont   intellectual   church and state

Choose words from the Word Bank to complete the sentences below. One word is not used at all.

1. American money is based on the _____, which is based on the number
   ten.

2. Jefferson's home, Monticello, is located in the _____ area of Virginia.

3. The belief that the government should not get involved in people's religious beliefs is called the

CRITICAL THINKING

As you read, check off the roles that Jefferson played in his life.

___ writer	___ bricklayer	___ sailor	___ violinist
___ architect	___ president	___ professor	___ ambassador to England
___ soldier	___ painter	___ inventor	___ governor
___ lawyer	___ surveyor	___ actor	___ secretary of state
___ surgeon	___ Father of the University of Virginia		

USING PRIMARY SOURCES

WITH A PARENT OR PARTNER Thomas Jefferson wrote the Virginia Statute for Religious Freedom. It was a law that gave people in Virginia the right to worship in any religion they chose. Here are some words from the law. Read them with a parent or partner. Circle any words you don't know and look them up in a dictionary.

> no man shall be compelled to frequent or support any religious worship, place or ministry whatsoever, nor shall be . . . restrained, . . .or burdened in his body or goods, nor shall otherwise suffer on account of his religious opinions or belief . . . ; but that all men shall be free to profess, and by argument to maintain, their opinion in matters of religion, and that the same shall in no wise diminish . . .or affect their civil capacities.

This law guarantees that people

    a. may worship wherever they please

    b. will not lose government jobs because of their religious beliefs

    c. will not be arrested because of their religious beliefs

    d. will not lost property because of their religious beliefs

    e. All of the above

WITH A PARENT OR PARTNER

"Civil " comes from the Latin "civilis." In five minutes, write down all the words or phrases you can think of with the same root as "civil." Ask a parent or partner to do the same. Then read your lists to each other.

A PHILADELPHIA WELCOME
SUMMER IN PHILLY

SUMMARY James Madison and the other delegates to the Constitutional Convention met in Philadelphia to create a new plan of government.

ACCESS

What do you know about the Constitutional Convention? In your history journal, copy the K-W-L chart from page 8. In the first column, write everything you know about the Convention. Skim the chapters. Then, in the second column, write down what you still want to find out. As you read through the next few chapters, write notes in the final column, "What I Learned."

WORD BANK   imposing   Virginia Plan   median   friction   Framers

Choose words from the word bank to complete the sentences below. One word is not used at all.

1. The _____ age of Americans at the time of the Constitutional Convention was only sixteen.

2. The men who wrote the U.S. Constitution are called its _____.

3. At five feet six inches, James Madison was not at first glance an _____ man.

4. Before the convention started, Madison wrote a proposal for the Constitution called the

   _____.

5. Write the word that you did not use in a sentence.

_____

CRITICAL THINKING

COMPARE AND CONTRAST The sentences below describe James Madison, Thomas Jefferson, and Benjamin Franklin. In your history journal, copy the model of the three-circle Venn diagram below, but make it much bigger. Label each circle with one person's name. Now copy the phrases below in the correct circles. The phrases that apply to only one character go in that person's circle. The phrases that describe two people go in the area where the two circles belonging to those two characters connect. Any descriptions of all three belong in the central area formed by all three circles.

Delegate to Continental Congress   Founding Father

Delegate to Constitutional Convention   Father of the Constitution

Virginian   College-educated

Philadelphian   Self-educated

Scientist   Intellectual

Writer   President of the United States

Inventor

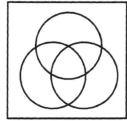

Three-circle Venn diagram

USING PRIMARY SOURCES

WITH A PARENT OR PARTNER When he was a young man, Benjamin Franklin wrote the following humorous epitaph for himself. (An epitaph is an inscription on a gravestone.) Read it and then answer the questions with a parent or a partner.

> The Body of
> B. Franklin, Printer;
> (Like the Cover of an old Book,
> Its Contents torn out
> And stript of its lettering and Gilding)
> Lies here, Food for Worms,
> But the Work shall not be lost;
> For it will, (as he beliv'd) appear once more,
> In a new and more elegant Edition
> Revised and corrected,
> By the Author.

1. This poem is a long simile. A simile makes a comparison between two unlike things using "like" or "as." To what is Franklin comparing his dead body?

_____

2. What are the "Contents" of the book?

    a. Ben Franklin's written essays   b. Ben Franklin's inner spirit or soul   c. A popular novel

3. Franklin imagines God as

    a. A book   b. A printer   c. An author

1. What is the "new and more elegant edition" of the work?

_____

CHAPTER 37

A SLAP ON THE BACK

SUMMARY Delegates disagreed about the new constitution. Some thought it should give the states more power. Some thought it should give more power to a central government. They compromised by creating a central government with shared powers.

ACCESS

In your history journal, create a main idea map graphic organizer with two smaller boxes. In the largest box, write, "Types of Government." In one of the smaller boxes, write "Confederation." In the other, write "Federation." Make three lines coming out from each smaller box. Write down three facts about each on the lines as you read this chapter.

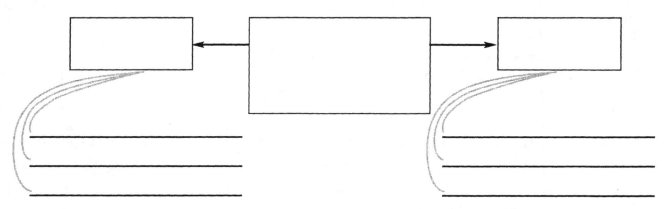

WORD BANK   confederation   federation   federalism   federal

Choose words from the Word Bank to complete the sentences below. One word is not used at all.

1. James Madison wanted a _____. This is a form of government that divides

    power between a central government and the states.

2. John Dickinson favored a _____. This is a partnership between the state

    and central governments.

3. The national government based in Washington, D.C. is called the _____

    government.

4. Write the word you did not use in a sentence.

    _____

WORD PLAY

The prefix "con" means means "with," or "together." Look for words in this chapter that begin with "con." Write them down here.

_____

_____

Now look them up in a dictionary. Which words come from the Latin root "con" or "com" plus another word? _____

Which words do not? _____

CRITICAL THINKING

WHO AM I? Use the name bank to identify the people described below. One name is not used.

NAME BANK   Benjamin Franklin   Robert Morris   James Wilson   John Rutledge
Gouverneur Morris   Alexander Hamilton   John Dickinson   James Madison

1. I am a delegate from Pennsylvania. I believe in democracy and think that individual rights are more important than property rights. _____

2. I am a delegate from New York. I want a strong central government and a powerful president.

   _____

3. I am a delegate from Pennsylvania. I wrote and edited the final draft of the Constitution.

   _____

4. I am a delegate from Pennsylvania. I am the richest man in Philadelphia.

   _____

5. I am a delegate from Virginia. I want to divide power between the state and federal governments.

   _____

6. I am a delegate from Delaware. I want most of the power to reside in the states.

   _____

7. I am a delegate from Pennsylvania. I am the oldest delegate to the convention.

   _____

WRITING

When two people compromise, each one must give up a little of what they want in order to reach an agreement they both like. Write about a real or imaginary situation in which you had to compromise. It could involve choosing which movie to see with a friend. It might involve sharing a room with a brother or sister.

CHAPTER 38 ROGER TO THE RESCUE

SUMMARY Big and little states argued about representation in the legislature. Roger Sherman made a proposal that became known as the Great Compromise.

ACCESS

Graphic organizers help us remember important information. In your history journal, make a chart with three columns. At the top of the first column, write "The Virginia Plan." At the top of the second, write "The New Jersey Plan." At the top of the third, write "The Great Compromise." As you read the chapter, write down important facts about each plan for the Constitution.

WORD BANK   grievances   orator   The Great Compromise

Choose words from the Word Bank to complete the sentences below.

1. The Declaration of Independence includes a list of complaints, or _____, against King George II.

2. Gouverneur Morris was a brilliant _____ who delivered spellbinding speeches at the convention.

3. _____ provided for a two-house legislature.

CRITICAL THINKING

FACT OR OPINION A fact is a statement that can be proven. An opinion judges things or people, but it cannot be proved or disproved. Some sentences below are facts and others are opinion. Write "F" in front of the facts and "O" in front of the opinions.

__1. "The New Jersey Plan was introduced by William Paterson."

__2. "The Virginia Plan . . . favored the states with the most people: Virginia, Massachusetts, and Pennsylvania."

__3. "It seemed that a constitution would never get written."

__4. "Sherman was a tough old Connecticut Yankee."

__5. "The Constitutional Convention needed a man of good sense and few words."

__6. "Roger Sherman had signed the Declaration of Independence and the Articles of Confederation."

__7. "The New Jersey Plan . . . meant that Delaware, with 59,000 people, would have the same number of congressmen as Virginia, with almost 692,000."

__8. "[Roger Sherman] is the oddest shaped character I ever remember to have met with."

WRITE ABOUT IT

In your history journal, write a dramatic scene set in the Indian Queen tavern. Two delegates are talking about the Virginia Plan and the New Jersey Plan. One should be from a big state and one from a little state. Other delegates hear them and join in. The conversation becomes quite heated. Use the information from the chart you created for the "Access" section. Work with a parent or partner, or a group if you can.

CHAPTER 39

JUST WHAT IS A CONSTITUTION?

SUMMARY The Constitution is the supreme, or highest, law of the United States of America. It can only be changed by amendments.

ACCESS

Do you know the names of your two senators and your congressional representative? If you don't, look them up on the Internet or in your school library. Write the names in your history journal.

WORD BANK   check and balance   ratified   supreme law   amendments

Complete the paragraph below by writing the words and phrases from the Word Bank in the blanks. One phrase is not used at all.

The Framers wrote the Constitution to be the _____ of the land. It

provides for three branches of government that _____ the power of the other .

_____, or changes, to the Constitution must be approved by Congress and

_____ by three-quarters of the state legislatures.

WORD PLAY
The word "supreme" has the same root as "super." With a parent or partner, write down as many words as you can think of that begin with "super" or "supra." Compare lists. Look up any that are unfamiliar. Are the meanings of the words similar? How?

_____

CRITICAL THINKING

COMPARE AND CONTRAST These phrases describe the roles and responsibilities of the three branches of the federal government. Sort the phrases into three columns, "Executive," "Legislative," and "Judicial," " in a chart in your history journal.

Imposes taxes

Commands the army and navy

Makes laws

Divided into two lawmaking bodies

Makes sure laws are carried out fairly

Checks the power of the other branches

Headed by a supreme court

Carries out laws

Runs federal court system

Declares wars

Headed by one person

Votes on amendments to Constitution

USING PRIMARY SOURCES

ANALYSIS Look at the picture of the United States official seal on page 174. Every part of the seal is a symbol of the nation somehow.

1. What does the eagle stand for?

2. What is the eagle holding in its claws?_____ What do they stand for?

_____

3. Which part(s) of the seal represents the thirteen states?_____

4. Why is the eagle's body covered with a shield?_____

5. Why are beams shining out from the clouds?_____

6. In a sentence or two, explain the meaning of the seal as a whole.

_____

_____

WORD PLAY What other word has the same root as the Latin "Pluribus"?

_____

CHAPTER 40

GOOD WORDS AND BAD

SUMMARY The Constitution did not give the same rights to women, enslaved people, and Indians the same rights as to white men who owned property. However, the words "We, the people" seemed to promise that some day they would receive those rights.

ACCESS

Think back a few chapters to the discussion of compromise. Lawmakers must often compromise on issues in order to pass a law. In a newspaper or magazine, find an issue on which people disagree. Discuss both sides with a parent or partner.

WORD BANK   Preamble   cotton gin   diabolical   slave trade

Choose words from the word bank to complete the sentences below. One word is not used at all.

1. The Constitution stated that the _____ could not be outlawed until 1808.

2. The introduction, or _____, to the Constitution begins with the words "We, the People."

3. The invention of the _____, in 1783 separated the cotton seeds from the fibers.

Read the definition of the word you did not use on page 181. Then write it in a sentence.

_____

CRITICAL THINKING

CAUSE AND EFFECT Creating a constitution involved many decisions and compromises. Match the "causes" in the right-hand column with the "effects" in the right hand column. (There is one extra effect.)

Cause

1. The Framers knew they had to create a Constitution that all Americans would approve

2. Settlers wanted Indian lands

3. The citizens of South Carolina and Georgia would not approve the Constitution if it prohibited slavery

4. George Mason knew the South was not ready to eliminate slavery

5. The South would not agree to eliminate the slave trade immediately

6. Eli Whitney invented the cotton gin

Effect

a. SO he backed a plan to outlaw the slave trade instead.

b. SO the delegates compromised on a plan to eliminate the slave trade in twenty years.

c. SO slavery became profitable again.

d. SO they were forced to compromise on many issues.

e. SO the Framers did not devise a plan to share land with the Indians.

f. SO George Washington would not sign the Constitution.

g. SO the delegates allowed slavery to continue.

USING PRIMARY SOURCES

Some delegates argued against slavery or the slave trade at the convention. Read the following passages with a parent or a partner. Then answer the questions.

Luther Martin of Maryland:

[The slave trade] was inconsistent with the principles of the revolution, and dishonorable to the American character.

George Mason of Virginia:

Slavery discourages arts and manufactures. The poor despise labor when performed by slaves. They prevent the immigration of whites. . . . They produce the most [harmful] effect on manners. Every master of slaves is born a petty tyrant.

1. Which writer is against slavery for practical reasons? _____

2. Which writer is against slavery as a matter of principle? _____

3. Why do you think slavery might "discourage arts and manufactures"?

_____

4. Why do you think slavery might have a "[harmful] effect on manners"?

_____

5. Mason considers the harmful effect of slavery on all of the following EXCEPT
   a. the slaves.   b. poor white workers.   c. the slave owners.   d. the economy of the South.

NAME _____

LIBRARY / MEDIA CENTER RESEARCH LOG

DUE DATE _____

What I Need to **Find**

I need to use:

☐ primary
☐ secondary sources.

Places I **Know** to Look

Brainstorm: Other Sources and Places to Look

WHAT I FOUND

Title/Author/Location (call # or URL)

☐ Book/Periodical
☐ Website
☐ Other

☐☐ ☐☐ ☐☐ ☐☐ ☐☐ ☐☐ ☐☐
☐☐ ☐☐ ☐☐ ☐☐ ☐☐ ☐☐ ☐☐
☐☐ ☐☐ ☐☐ ☐☐ ☐☐ ☐☐ ☐☐

☐ Primary Source
☐ Secondary Source

☐ Suggestion
☐ Library Catalog
☐ Browsing
☐ Internet Search
☐ Web link

How I Found it

Rate each source from 1 (low) to 4 (high) in the categories below

helpful

relevant

LIBRARY/ MEDIA CENTER RESEARCH LOG

NAME _____

DUE DATE _____

What I Need to **Find**

I need to use:

- ☐ primary sources.
- ☐ secondary

Brainstorm: Other Sources and Places to Look

Places I **Know** to Look

WHAT I FOUND

Title/Author/Location (call # or URL)

	How I Found it					Rate each source from 1 (low) to 4 (high) in the categories below	
Book/Periodical	Website	Other	Primary Source	Secondary Source	Suggestion · Library Catalog · Browsing · Internet Search · Web link	helpful	relevant

CPSIA information can be obtained
at www.ICGtesting.com
Printed in the USA
BVHW061006300419
546939BV00001B/2/P